LITTLE SILVER

Jane Griffiths was born in Exeter in 1970, and brought up in Holland and Devon. After reading English at Oxford, where her poem 'The House' won the Newdigate Prize, she worked as a book-binder in London and Norfolk. Returning to Oxford, she completed her doctorate on the Tudor poet John Skelton and worked on the Oxford English Dictionary for two years. After teaching English Literature at St Edmund Hall, Oxford, and then at the universities of Edinburgh and Bristol, she now teaches at Wadham College, Oxford, and is literary editor of the *Oxford Magazine*.

She won an Eric Gregory Award for her poetry in 1996. Her book *Another Country: New & Selected Poems* (Bloodaxe Books, 2008), which included a new collection, *Eclogue Over Merlin Street* (2008), together with large selections from two previous Bloodaxe collections, *A Grip on Thin Air* (2000) and *Icarus on Earth* (2005), was shortlisted for the Forward Prize for Best Collection. Her later collections from Bloodaxe are *Terrestrial Variations* (2012), *Silent in Finisterre* (2017), a Poetry Book Society Recommendation, and *Little Silver* (2022).

Her academic books include *John Skelton and Poetic Authority: Defining the Liberty to Speak* (Oxford University Press, 2006) and *Diverting Authorities: Experimental Glossing Practices in Manuscript and Print* (Oxford University Press, 2014). She also co-edited the study *Architectural Space and the Imagination: Houses in Literature and Art from Classical to Contemporary* (Palgrave, 2020) with Adam Hanna.

JANE GRIFFITHS

Little Silver

BLOODAXE BOOKS

Copyright © Jane Griffiths 2022

ISBN: 978 1 78037 612 7

First published 2022 by
Bloodaxe Books Ltd,
Eastburn,
South Park,
Hexham,
Northumberland NE46 1BS

www.bloodaxebooks.com
For further information about Bloodaxe titles
please visit our website and join our mailing list
or write to the above address for a catalogue.

Supported using public funding by
**ARTS COUNCIL
ENGLAND**

Cover design: Neil Astley & Pamela Robertson-Pearce.

Printed in Great Britain by Bell & Bain Limited, Glasgow, Scotland, on
acid-free paper sourced from mills with FSC chain of custody certification.

Say goodbye to her, to the Alexandria you are losing.

C.P. CAVAFY, 'The God Abandons Antony'

ACKNOWLEDGEMENTS

Acknowledgements are due to the editors of *Ash Magazine*, Chough Books, *ORB* and http://plague20journal.com for publishing some of these poems.

CONTENTS

Waking,

the book you were reading called *Night* still
fly-leaved to your fingers, the bedside
light casting shadows like bison running at full
stretch for centuries now, you know of course
you have been dreaming of the cave's wide
mouth and a small boat negotiating
the underground stream to its receding source:
you have the word *bark* on your tongue,
the root of it twisted and solid in the shifty room
as the thick of the current, the needlepoint
eye of the creature in the eye of the hunt, or the storm.

Inscape

What was it he saw in that long split
second when the solid rock opened to show
its workings and he went feet first

into the grassed-over, half-forgotten shaft
feeling himself suddenly very small
and divided, one eye as it was, level

with the choughs, taking in the bracken's
rusty cut and thrust, the dazzling elisions
of sea and sky where he whistled out of tune

the way he'd done since time immemorial,
the other up against the granite – the mica,
the seams and grain of it, and the scars?

Was it the truth of the matter, an abstract
of human hands excavating the surface,
centuries of human labour extracting ore,

living through and under the earth, or one
of the stories we tell ourselves about our
selves, one of the parables we pass on

in that long split second under the sky's
blue seal, provisional, before a rucksack
breaks – or fails to break – the fall?

The Drowning at Porthcurno

So this girl, sixteen and elver in her skin goes down
to the sea to test its boundaries where it dances
bejewelled & beau-jangled in turquoise cobalt and emerald
and turns out its pockets over & over on the cove's
       silver sand

where she takes a turn with it, rises and falls on its full
skirts out past the breakers: it's simple, she thinks,
to fall and rise with it: natural as breathing, on and on –
Only, she's left her ring, her grandmother's gold one
       with emerald brilliants

back up the beach in a bag against the milk-wooded
cliff where she saw the play last night, actors leaning out
on the wind over the edge above the sea-song so she caught
her breath – she'll go and fetch it, she thinks, since the sands
       are packed with people

and easy to reach. Only, the breakers turn & turn her
and she laughs, treading the effervescent water and waving
to a boy not three yards away on dry land who throws a ball
for his small black dog that dashes & dashes into the sea-spume
       and out again –

but she can't do it, there's an undertow, so she dances on
the spot and the breakers turn & turn her and though
she still smiles she is going under, toes dragged in the long
silt nets of the waves as their sheer green glide pulls her
       away

from the shore and the green glade where she will blindly
follow a man she barely knows and blindly lie down
with him, trusting to the earth to hold her, away from

her plane's slick slipstream through the suddenly potholed
       & unsteadfast air,

from the black spin of ice under her wheels, from the sun's
sheen on the fourth-floor sashes she'll throw open in
Kentish Town –
                It pulls her under and round
through the sleek gold ring of herself and all its endings
       & all the lives before

though the beach is no more than three yards away
and she sees them standing there: her parents, brother,
and daughter who'll never be born now, unconcernedly
stepping over sandcastles as she opens her mouth to call
       and takes in water, and disbelief –

as, in myth, women slip from their skins into an unknown element

Only, there's a hand round her arm and she is hooked
and landed fish-like at the feet of a man who is not
her father and they look hard at each other for a moment
before she turns and heads back up the beach for her bag
       that's waiting under the cliff.

Off-spring

Out above the pool, each time the black and white
film rolls the girl starts forward on the springboard,
stutters a bit as she slips from frame to frame. Feet
tense against its buoyancy, she casts off –
 her self wholly

in her body as the world swings through 150 degrees
around her. Foetal, she furls, then stretches for the water
that parts for her fingertips' sub-aqueous progress
and all that follows
     when we pause
        rewind –
          and here
  she goes again

following her footprints to their promised up and over until
this slip, this decisive flicker of refusal as she stands for all
the mothers and their mothers before them who carried
daughters proud of their solitudes, whose sons were vital
   permission to leave off –

and *oh*, we ask, *is this a negative?* – as the girl, paused on the rim
of the board that's kicking with her weight watches her friends
on the far side scry for their children, one hand to their eyes,
the other raising the flag of hope that springs eternal in the form
   of pale blue swim-shorts,

and singular, turns out of the picture and says 'Take five?'

The Amortals

I

Bored with the long school holiday Miles
sidles into the studio, amateur ornithologist
            complete with guide to once

common or garden birds – house sparrow, chaffinch,
blue jay. *Blue*, he says, *as in electric*, idly
            swinging binoculars

from their long strap, idly running a hand along
the backs of the canvases, spelling out the names:

> Self-Portrait with Flora and Miles
> Flora and Miles in Edinburgh
> Flora with Elizabeth, Miles with Joan
> Spitalfields with Flora and Miles
> Flora and Miles with Smokey
> Flora and Miles in Drag
> Flora and Miles at Home

Mum, he says, *why are we in all your pictures?*
For focus, I say, for the human scale. Idly,
            finger blearing the charcoal.

So if we didn't exist you'd have had to invent us?
Yes, I say, something like that.

II

Today Flora and Miles are learning about war –
how it happens in other places
      over the water,

how people put out to sea in little boats
under a flag-like blue and gold sky
      of stars.

Flora says she sees them sailing for the idea
of a green continent unrolling, unbombsites rising
      from uncratered plains

where they'll walk long roads lined by unexplosions
(lamp-posts, trees) and she sees them sinking in
      a watery horizon

that towers infinitely too close to hand.
She says if she sits very still under the table
      and saves her money

she'll come to understand. Miles, practical,
will make a raft: he gathers water bottles,
      murmurs words

like *buoyancy* and *inflatable* under his breath,
exhales slow. Flora considers the solid ring
      of hills round the town.

Miles says if it happens we'll take the raft over
to Exwick, live on apples and fish & chips
      and be on Sky

like the *Titanic*, he says, hands full of improvised
flotation devices, or like all the stars going out
      that we did last week at school.

III

Flora and Miles have discovered perspective:
how the ringing we hear from our garden above
      the river is real

and marks a school whose iron bell's still
in its cut-out enclosure. We reach it by walking
      across the water,

stand under it to see how the building's whole –
and grey stone, like ours. And here the voices
      we hear rising

from valley playground to high horizon are tagged
to bodies in a life-size crocodile stepping out
      through the yeasty air

past the fleet of lorries that deliver Mother's Pride
and the metal five-seater *dragon* (says Flora)
      horse (says Miles)

shepherded by teachers with names like Mrs Wade,
Mr Dorridge, Mr Penwill, Miss Clare and Miss Ousebury –
      shorthand for humans

tall as angels, briefcases hugged to their hearts
enclosing their inner lives –
      like angels, but not identical.

We could have lived here, says Miles, we'd have been
not at St David's and known the bodies whose voices
      are flying upward

(and dragon's teeth, says Flora, whole rows of them).
The field where they found that girl would have been
      the field we played

spinning bike wheels, sun early dark, the bell speaking
in tongues – it's hard to tell where we'd be now,
   out past the edge of town.

  IV

Flora and Miles are winged today –
   fully fledged, sweeping off

live heads of geraniums in the garden
   room – slowly – learning

to adjust their balance, their sudden
   want of gravity.

In the kitchen they rise like balloons
   on helium, toes dragging

the worktop and almost weightless
   unaccustomed bulk jamming

the doorframe – once, twice, then
   free to the length

of the garden that's the length
   of summer and unseen

till past tea-time when Miles is found
   upside-down, hook-kneed

in the apple tree, wing tips just brushing
   the ground in

intricate feathery geometries.
      Flora's flat out

on a limb, tired she says from treading
      air above Bury Meadow

with its stone pinecone-tipped gate posts
      and inhospitable birches,

and from holding hands with the clock-tower,
      though she denies

having crossed the New North Road –
      not so far, she says.

On her phone, Miles on the pepperpot
      spire of St David's.

On Miles' phone, Flora in the shade
      of the tallest angel

with a broken bird, her arms a cradling
      of feather and bone.

V

Flora and Miles are asking about their father – why,
when I paint him, it's with his back to us, holding
      a curtain slant

against the light and looking out across the park.
You paint the beech tree in more detail, they say,
      which is true.

Is it because he's in Bristol?
Is it because he's abroad?

Is it because you didn't really know him or because
he was always on the verge of being someone
            other, and always

moving that you paint him so still, on his own,
a totem down the edge of the picture that's only
            gesturally human?

Is it because he was short that you paint him so tall?

   VI
Flora and Miles want to know *what was it like before us?*
so I tell them the river at Blackfriars, early, the bridge
            on sunfretted girders

and St Paul's weathervane an exclamation of light.
The river-crossing, daily: velvet coat and beret and a canvas
            holdall of knives

sharp as the city's four dimensions, the here and now of it.
Passing light-foot up Holborn with a head full of box wood,
            leather, loose-leaf gold –

the world material. The world in gauge and estimate:
lick and spit on the shanks of a small brass alphabet,
            a graver's pin-prick

rule of thumb – and each wood-block and book-block
adding something to the weight of it.
                        The press of air

            between people crossing

with their lives in their hands, quick and in the making.
The phrase *in the thick of things*. Wanting a medium for it.
      Buying a plan-chest at the Elephant.

Underground, I read 'two girls cross the bridge, hatless,
they triumph' and 'tulips as shriek-marks, yelps of delight'.
      I read 'yesterday I walked

into a post-box, yesterday –' and there was a gap of years.

      *

Your father wanted you, said it would be easy as calling you
in from the garden – *Bluebell, Ebenezer* (*imagine*, says Miles) –
      and I rode the top deck

of a bus in Oxfordshire over the wheaten lie of the land,
imagined your weight, the division, my eyes in your faces,
      his eyes in mine –

Imagined you pointing – *Look, two hares! Look, a deer running, no –*
a deer stopped dead – and the dark wood untouched, in embryo,
      and all the books unbound

or the three of us at the kitchen table and how you'd ask just
that question. 'But,' Flora says, 'We wouldn't have been like *this*,
      you know.' 'Oh yes,' I say, 'I do.'

VII

Flora is home from her fourth driving lesson,
her first out of town. They went north, she says,
  up the incline

by the nursery and along to Ide through lanes
where she felt the pressing weight of hedges darkly
  edging the corn

(why *ears*, she asks, is it because of Midas?)
then along the open stretch to the railway bridge,
  fast, she says, at 50,

though it was somehow slow the way the fields
rolled back on themselves: like old film,
  like when we flew

and I felt so close to the ground I knew the map
of this island, England, the kingdom – you name it –
  like the bones in my hand:

roads breeding roads, knowing I could go anywhere.
It was like dreaming new rooms in our house
  or like in school

writing right up to and off the edges of the paper.
Is that how you felt when you were learning?
  Open-ended, I say. Of course.

VIII

Flora and Miles want to know *where did we come from?*
so I tell them, from Lodge Hill, Little Silver,
       Bury Meadow and Little Knowle,

from ghost stories at Christmas, conkers in October,
birch-light in spring. From your father's love of possession,
       from your father's love,

and out of my head with its repetition, repetition, fear
of refusal, its idea of home: a yellow lamp in the kitchen,
       your footsteps down the hall

centripetal (which is what you say with roses). From unspoken
promises, marks in the indecipherables of our palms; also
       from a coffee cup

slammed hard against the ceiling and its slow sepia seedhead
stain. From the blue cat dancing paw-to-paw with its shadow
       dead on the road,

from my hands writing white and always at one remove.
From fairground music, from a bed under a skylight
       raising the roof –

From events tethering sky to earth, from the self
that centres your father. From all of this.
       From none of the above.

IX

Bored with the long vacation Flora
sidles into the studio, experimental
          electric hair streaking

across the window as if a passing jay –
How do people believe in God, she asks, idly
          running a hand along

the tops of the canvases, idly checking
for dust and eyeing up the names:

Flora and Miles in St Werburghs (The Allotments)
Flora and Miles down Cot Valley (Feeding Ostriches)
Flora and Miles at Nancherrow (Not Feeding the Donkeys)
Flora, Miles and goldfinches at Gilgarran
Flora and Miles in People's Park
          (in Bury Meadow, by the Albert Hall)
Flora, Miles and Troy (Distons Lane)
Flora, Miles and telescope at Bliss Mill
Flora, Miles, and the absent lilies of Lily Brook
Flora and Miles by the hollow oak
Landscape without Flora and Miles

Mum, she says, *why are we in all your pictures?*
For focus, I say. For what might have been. Idly,
          watching her face in the glass.

So if we existed the tree could stand alone?
Yes, I say. That's it, more or less.

Distance Lane

Far from the farmer who didn't give it his name
from the long dead mill-workers' Paradise and Bliss
from the old tannery and its patient horses
          in black and white and sepia
          and 2hp traffic in skins

from my neighbours' chalk feet on blackboard gravel
the hooded woman who crosses to the other side
from the Baptists' total immersion in sawing,
          sandblasting, vehicles vocally reversing
          and never a day of rest

a slip of the pen delivers us – from Distons to Distance –
as if (at the end of an old tale) all's exactly as it was, but.

Here are the hooded neighbours, the gravel-voiced woman
in her chalk-white TT, the buzzing roofs of a rest home
behind the Apiary, and by the railway's lost tracks
          two children, rubber-booted
          and serious, waiting to meet us

          or just waiting to wave as we pass.

Foundling

The way he came was not by river.
There was no basket, no cradling
in bulrush, only the singing

black parallels that conjoined
at Paddington – so many lines
back to so many different lives.

No note, fine linen, real child.
A little gold. He worked the railway.
But when he told his own sons

one day his ship would come home,
it was as if he were watching some
tall three-master, sails furled, slip

silently through night-time London
to dock at Star Street, all his possible
histories under wraps in its hold.

Lifelines

I

The Queen Anne's lace in the hedges is dead.
On the edge of the sea-mist crocosmia,
heather and convolvulus shade off as *this*
shades into last summer and its previous:
green, lavish, stalking into the mist.
The cropped oak on the edge of the visible
is a stoppage, a point of rest in the self-
coloured non-dimensional blank

that is mist, that is

the work before the work is properly begun –

a foreconceit –

And you ask me, where are the children?

II

All summer face down in the bracken-
scrubbed granite of the carn I've dreamed
your necklaces: topaz, amethyst, tiger's eye

and pearl. The hand-me-downs, you said,
regal against your pillows over marmite soldiers,
and we'd repeat: *sapphire for Mary, diamond*

for Anne, opal for Hannah, emerald for Jane.
All summer on the carn I've dreamed refrain –
how many things we contrive to hold together

in time. Here, on the coast-road, the penned
cattle four-square and bullish, the unpenned
cattle nose to tail under a sky in sapphire, opal.

There, your hands ringed gold on the covers,
Grandad with the tea-cups, silk-dressing-gowned.

The sea breezing in with a kind of mistiness,
we go under laughing, as children do –

All summer on the carn the high horizon.

The sky calling us back down to earth.

III

In Holland, very young, I stumbled on a necklace,
or the shape of one, stretched in mud at the edge
of a ditch of standing water: light-gilt, etched,

enamelled, just lipping the surface. Standing
by the edge of the water with a bent stick
I clutched the word *treasure* tight to my chest

even as a solid shaft of sun shifted and dissolved
the links, each one: the gold filigree, the bezel-set
pearls and my crooked fist closing on them

and angling through. Grasping for a weight
and coming up with duckweed, arms streaming
beauty-spots: iridescent green and maculate.

IV

In London, very young, you had the habit
of trees, petticoats frilling the branches.

You lost a brother to the Somme,
three small sisters to nothing in particular.

You scissored through your last-but-one
sister Annie's cast-off silk, gathered its green

Grecian swathes with a safety-pin –
and when she complained, you shared,

two heads and one dress, turn and turn
about, as if two hearts and just one tune.

Improvise, you said. Make do and mend.

Your last surviving sister took half your name.

You lost Annie in the Blitz, to pneumonia.

V

In this photograph, your sleek-haired sons turn
formally to the light, though one went on

to break all the limbs he had; the other, bucked
by the tree he was pruning, flew backwards (you said)

as if lassoed, past the window where you stood
half-washed plate in hand and hand to mouth.

You scarcely signed your work. Sometimes three
scrat initials on the unglazed underside of a bowl.

Sometimes none. Your fingers teased the colours
of your garden from bare earth: emerald, gold,

agate, peridot. Each spring its aureate
sap filled the veins of strawberries and roses.

Each winter you spoke their names – bifold,
Latinate – over the beds where they lay orderly

in their dirt-velvet chambers: latent jewels
like sons, daughters-in-law, grandchildren.

Each year more and more, like refrain.

VI

I dreamed I was reaching for a book
and you asked, where are the children?
The work undone.

I dreamed the shape of the work swimming
to the surface, the way on a potter's wheel
object and idea fall together.

I dreamed your sisters: Annie, Lily, Edith.
The hour's life of the twins baptised by tea-cup –
your father grasping for the nearest names.

I dreamed three sisters, Annie, Lily, Lilian,
auburn-haired and in white, lace skimming
hedges and bracken, hands full of daisy-chains,

hazel-eyed. I dreamed the silences between.

I dreamed you were digging your garden
in a sensible skirt, fork in hand –
so very down to earth.

I dreamed you were digging your garden
and it was coming up pearls.

VII

I'm not clear about sequences, how one thing leads to another. The catch is repetition, or variation – one and the same. And how, when there is no child, to imagine the shape of one. What's the setting for her? A tenement on Star Street? A swing above a stream? Is she in fancy dress – piratical, or with a queeny coronet? There's no life without a medium – which is the thing itself, or so I say, living mostly through representations. Though if the work covers for the child, what does the child cover for?

VIII

All summer I've dreamed your necklaces, triple
branched pendants of daisy, marguerite and pearl.
I've dreamed myself empty-handed.

All summer I've been making necklaces – silver
and sea-glass. Gold. And you ask how I account –

No, no children, but sentences and findings.

Your hands, spinning the pot on its wheel
upwards and into thin air. Your necklace
ending in bricolette, a single pearl –

No, no children.
                        No, it is not a grief –
or only as a pot contains the negative of itself.

In the three rooms of this cliff-top house
on the edge of a sea of mist, opalescent,
I've been considering the doublet

mother and child – the rhythm of it
unanswerable, an end in itself.
And the shapes of our lives –

my plain to your pearl.
                        No, it is not a grief –

I've your ropes of gold, simple catches.

In an envelope, a snip of our auburn hair.

CODA

She left, they say, *a considerable body of work.*
No, she said, *this was a make that didn't work.*
Thank you, he wrote, *for your interest in my work.*

Child, chain, book – the self's evidence of itself,
the body's casts that stand like signs in stone
in proof of the ice age or that Shaun loves Ange.

Ye know eke that in forme of speche is chaunge –

all summer I've been looking back at the staggered
houses on the rim of the carn, the carn staggered
above the houses. The house the body beside

the body, the house the work falling ruin for
centuries turned in human picking over human
life – then unwitnessed, alien, a heap of stone

where sea mews, or something very like, nest all

summer   silver

                        bone or pearl

                                     lace, nameless

the carn

          the sea

                    mist

                           unseen

                                              mews

Isolation

As it might be, a sea-mist.
A lighthouse, with nothing to say but in saying it
finding its beam is broadly contemporary.

As it might be, a chance perspective: small boats
imperially holding six feet off from shore – or,
empirically, a distance of two metres.

The same sea-mist, meaning differently from before.
The houses' white-outs within the white-out
all together now, but separate –

or so someone might say, lightly, walking down
into it along the long lines of telegraph poles,
skirting a field of gulls that dip in and out

its furrows like a flock of waves under mist,
listening in on the infinite present of the world
all alone: the chatter and sough of it over

rock-fall at the foot of the cliff as it was and ever
shall be when these words speak to nothing,
when they are hieroglyph, when there is no one left

to say how in that time, the time of pestilence,
people looked for signs. And how the boats, the mist,
the coast and lighthouse were nothing, but.

Grace

(for Karen)

What's not accountable – as a homing pigeon
on the home stretch, half the arc of the world
under each wing, drops into its loft and sets
all the bells ringing in their hatches. A given
that's anything but: that sheer scintillating
surplus of sea as far as the eye – though here
on the face of it we want the word and grounds
to speak from, all the time building houses
of twig on the sand.
                It's as in conversation –
the spring and return of it, the lock unjammed,
or when a retriever comes belting up, dogged
and golden made flesh, offering two sticks for one –
so looking back, you say *there but for the –*
or, *it came*, you say, *out of the clear blue –*

Out of the Picture

(after Morwenna Thistlethwaite)

Whatever happens is happening to someone else:
the pain in the room I couldn't rightly say was mine,
so too the three neat children and their dolls' house.
The grey cat is here on my behalf to witness

how the table's set geometrically for tea
or chess, how the deep blue cloth shadows
the dusk-blue of the sky and the window
holds something in reserve behind its glass.

So this is what life looks like, just a little
at a distance: a bowl of oranges shored against
the double yellow of the road, a couple
on the verge whose shoulders' slant signals

part-communication – and a third, absorbed
as we too'd look absorbed if anyone thought
to record the sun's light study of our waiting rooms
where now and again things click into place

as cup to saucer, pawn to king's castle – or come
apart as in this watercolour of a TV dark
under the blooming life of a geranium, and two
small figures on the screen, running for their own.

Negative Space

Jess says we should concentrate on the visible
absences: the cloth's concavities between bowl
and jug. How the seeming ellipsis in that bone-

china handle's a slip where your finger comes
unstuck, the clear cut-out between cup and lip's
like the stair space a mistaking foot falls into

or the globe cracked up from Brazil to Nigeria.
She says, it's the squared-off wings of the cupola
that matter, not the bell bellying outward.

So the thing is this litter of glittery teardrops, not
the child, tongue between the tips of her teeth
in her mouth, ovoid, as she snips her ladies dancing

hand in hand across winter windows with their lights
punched out to show this space is what we inhabit,
papering bright stars over the enormous dark outside.

Snow and Privet

Her first snow and they were leaving
for good, they said – the two facts discrete
as single flakes dissolving on the tongue.

Hedges, hunch-backed, lent weight
to the word *giant*. The sky damped down.

It was very quiet.
                          And above all,

there was the snow
                                    the snow endlessly
unwriting itself
                          the snow laden on privet

its leaves braille-like
                                    coding the snow

the innumerable snow birds
                              slipping through her hands
(her clumsy gloves)

                          the privet's silent morse

the word *swan-song*

                          and that dented blue car wing
lodged in the hedge since before she was born:

                                    adrift, invisible (some long-
                                    forgotten accident)

the words (*cause* and *effect*) coming out wrong

Moving the House

Up for removal, this small wooden house is cut
loose from its footings and transported bodily
over twenty miles to stand in perfect

semblance of itself off the edge of the city's map.
A different quality of silence about it.
So too planes settle on tarmac.

So too pilgrims who emerge from under the wings
with out-of-kilter backpacks overbalancing
carry themselves lightly as if in transit

still, paused between descent and take-off in a place
whose nights are flocks of birds pulsing
like irregular star-signs that shear along

dotted lines and separate as they remember
not the path they've flown but where
they started from – the keeps

and coops of friable slats and chicken wire,
the memory cells they've banked on
since birth, today as ever

tumbling from the sky on the long leash of home only
to fall unerringly through the heart of the want
where the house is gone.

Little Silver

What would it mean to write a house on a hill,
to have that lucidity to start from – one word
following another as feet fall in a drift of
leaves, making out a pattern that is real
entirely as the path you summon to return
and the house in its airiness, its spring-boarded
corridor and view of a sky-bright slingback
of river – if it weren't for the trees, that is.
The path home always comes down to this:
Little Silver, what you were born with.

Little Silver, what you were born with:
a clutch of talents, a clearing in the wood.
A charm slipped under tree roots, promise –
kept, in that dream you have of pursuit
down red-brick terraces to sudden spaciness
where the road opens on long grass, silver birches,
and you pause in near-recognition, then escape
down a side-street you couldn't have made up.
If you could leave off here, you said –
Little Silver, a true and double passage.

Little Silver, a true and double passage.
A small gift of tongues to take you out
into the world's roundabout ways
and crossed purposes to talk of leaving,
to talk of anything but –
                              The house
on the hill always above and beyond the word,
impervious: its paper-white walls and indelible
ink roof-line drawing the eye through leaves
at the turn of the lane, where the sky's clearing –
Little Silver, the coin leading home.

Little Silver, the coin leading home
up the hill past the unhinged garages
of Taddiford and through its red stone arch
to a road slipper as a stream brimming over
or rain going under the stream: over, again.
If you could leave off here, you said –
Little Silver, what you come back to when
your own path home leads only to this:
[*a blank space*   ]
a little silvering between the trees.

A little silvering between the trees:
skylight where no light should be,
a level site and rubble that was the house
on the hill, its singing slate and blaze-
white gable, its wood-framed cavernousness.
The unselved space impossibly too small
for the house that you still see standing
above the valley, that you lift and lodge
in the eight rooms, store-cupboard, loft
and corridor of the heart. That you carry off

quietly down the hill, to Little Silver.

Coda
What would it mean to write a house on a hill,
to write it and see it standing: singly, without
overspill, to have that lucidity to start from?
Not to need the words for it, seeing it stand
alone, not to chase the shape of it through
the wood to the point there's no unknowing –
how its unbeing's blazed in black and white
between the trees.
                            And not to repeat this.
Not to turn from the shocked hole in the hill
to the broken charm that is Little Silver:

Little Silver, the long way home.
Little Silver, a kind of hedginess.
Little Silver, a name for the unknown.
Little Silver, the house in mind alone.
Little Silver, a feint and narrow passage
that's means to an end, a paper trail
back to the void of what you were born with.
The writing that won't put house and hill
together, the sleight of heart, safe house
that was never your own, and the silver
unleaving where you turn and leave off –

Gilgarran is the lost house on the hill.

Charm

to whom it may concern

May your hands meet handles where no doors are –
       smooth, round, perfectly fulfilling.
Safe in your concrete shell, may you hear boards creak
       the lost length of a corridor.
May a piano play between floors as you sleep.
May you know the pyracantha by pricking of your thumbs.
May you be visited by children.
Turning into the hill's beech-mast, leaf-drift, silver birch,
       may you see the house: black slate and white walls
       under the sign of its double gable.
May you know it for home.
May you be blind-sided for love of it.
May you meet my father in shorts and an orange shirt
       planting out the rockery on your first-floor landing.
May you meet my grandmother taking cuttings in the hall.
May her secateurs pass through your fingers.
May you be puzzled by the sough of wind through trees
       you've uprooted.
May you see a swing swinging in and out the vacuum
       framed by what you believe to be your walls.
May you know what you've done.
May you never know what's yours.
May the Bramley's crown stick in the throat of your stairs.
May your foundations be unaccountable.
May you step out, one day, into iris and lavender to hear
       (as if on a kite-string tuned to the wrong frequency):
We've put the cot and bureau in David's bedroom.
Where is it the steps go down to the lawn? There?
                     No, it's here.

Tall Story

This ten-year-old novelist in exile, non-pareil
scaler of trees who knows root and branch
of the hand-holds up the bank along Hollow Lane

> how to rig a rope swing
and the bucket and twist of it
> > the principles
of wattle & daub applied to an outlaw's den

but not how to articulate them, though she senses
names have a weight beyond the practical
and writes of a boy swept out to sea specifically

by the river Otter, the day the two of them walked
almost to Ladram Bay –
> > That novelist, sitting
at her grandmother's small oak desk with its fold-

down lid and very nearly secret drawer, imagines
take-off from a swing at its highest – her whole
body in italics *flying* the gap between its wooden

launch-pad and privet, feet angled against the sky
whose stars she links literal-mindedly to the foot
of her page, first tethering* then cutting them loose.**

She writes a bandstand, with *a clash of symbols*.
She writes the boy out of the river's mouth.
The birch by her window stands: untranslatably itself.

* *There are no trees in Holland so this didn't happen.*
** *If you look you'll see the hedge is still broken.*

Homily

(for George)

Take fireworks, for example, the morning
after: sherbet-pink sky-blue cardboard
carcasses staining the fresh fall of snow

and a handful of people, sticklike, in a riff
on the old song, stooping to recover them –
white breath
          a drift
                  white field –

and wanting to say 'This is really beautiful',
this first new year in a new country.
                     Just so –

though what will follow is all up in the air
      coin-like
             light-fingered
                     metamorph-
(o)
      hissing back down to earth.

Is fire work: one child cross-tongued, cross-
eyed with charcoal, drawing a blank. The other
reading about a foreign boy in a garden.

The old words ash in the mouth. One child
up a wooden tree in the yard, the other
reading about a boy in a foreign garden.

In the old house, the Bible open to the sky.
The parents turn over a text at random.
The names, one remove from their own.

The Silence

It has been so long.

This drift of white not a field.

Lost in the thick of the paper

I, a small upright.

A thin diagonal going forward angling
off a bit along the deckle of the horizon

Sometimes, signs for wings, or shelter
not joined up
vvv vvv

It's not clear how I came here.

The marks I left unfamiliar.

vvv

Whereof one cannot speak –

Therefore the loan of
another's speech in another's language

So long, the mother tongue

From London far

beyond the circumference of its easternmost mast
      the BBC turned pirate
      the signal going down with the sun
      the charts etherised at number 21

this wasn't London calling but London
talking to itself and the island's interior
while out beyond the North Sea's dark
radio silence we eavesdropped furiously
like children on the landing of life

just wanting to know where they'd begun

while then as now, lighthouses signalled serious
and particular dangers to freight ships charting
the tea-light leaf-dance of coastal towns now

as then and every night between below
the high fidelity of the stars

Anchorage

Who, who? asks an owl, caught
in the upturned bowl of night.

At the valley's end a neat
triangle of sea oscillates slightly.

Small granite houses along the ridge
are groundwork, silhouetted and steady,

so steady on their co-ordinates they
are a world away from the illuminated

ellipses off-shore that ride at anchor,
the botched craft that slip between

and behind them below the horizon
the full weight of the globe spinning

in its heavenly body of water, fringed
with thorny valleys like these. Only

when a cry goes up into the sky's
anechoic margin of error it means

differently in different human tongues.
And any which way, the next port of call.

Passage

Imagine a woman at her desk, an attic desk, writing
easily. The window is ajar. She has come upstairs

to shut the door on her life, its untidinesses.
At the centre of her island, around the end of a century,

she barely remembers the crossing, rocks tumbled like dice,
a scarlet life-belt spinning hoopla-style, and her father

calling to her in her mother tongue to jump, just jump through –

She is fifty, she knows a thing or two about belonging,

the daily return of the horizon and the way its treeline
jigsaws into sky: the off-black, off-white give and take of it.

The small wooden camel her son wedged behind the radiator
years ago now is not a ship crossing the desert. It is a small

wooden camel, undislodgeable. It was an accident.

When her eldest daughter asks her, in her mother's words,

for a true story she writes (easily) of rough white walls
and how the coast's 100 miles away or more –

of the children she has called into being
of a door closed

on passage through a needling forest
and the small wooden ship out at sea.

Fugue

This woman, cornered in the boat-train watching
the embankment's bramble and tangle-weed run through
the eyes in her reflected face that watch lights going up

upcountry and mark their settlements – dancers in the dark
dazzle that dances through and around the falling snow –

this is you in winter now,
                                         seeing also

you in winter past, having just got the hang of the trick –
which is to keep moving, balls of the feet centred on dye-
cast, die-hard and slightly divergent blades that hang

a right, then a left
                    (lift)

Left the reeds, right the town – low-rise, concrete, chimneyless –
the thing-not-there in your face as a cat or dog three-legged –

                    (lift)

Behind, the large pond you'll never learn to translate
                                         (*vijver*)
and other children on skates round a stall that sells off-white
polka brokken like enormous teeth where last night you spun

under Schiaparelli lights, six inches taller than on solid ground

                                         (right)
Now here you are doing a runner
                         no end in sight

left the reeds, right the town

(lift)

Under ice, fish frozen mid-turn are pale mooning orbs in
their orbits, your slipshod reflection not touching their open
mouths, open eyes haloed by scales that wink as you pass

(lift)

(The impossibility of death is years from being imagined)

Left behind the house on the hill, its hedges, trees, river

(lift)

Right grey brick paving and trying to invent (*river garden treasure*),
trying to lauch inflatables on this very pond as if the Amazon –

(right)

Here you duck for a small white bridge that divides one reach from
another – a tricky pass bringing neat white-booted feet together

        simultaneous   simultaneous
             toes facing front

(lift)

left the reeds   right the parting of lives
          so various

you on the boat-train

you distracted by likeness, always wanting the medium

you most desired as movement in middle distance

you learning the tongue as foreign body

                            body as foreign tongue

you scattering metalwork, paperwork, paper houses right & left

you dumb, you watching flame wrap the edge of a bookshelf
and spreading, you in close-up, brick wall in your face

you sharply exhaling on the sheer surface of gold leaf

you idling in corners, fingers numb and fingering keys

will never know how much time you don't have –

left the work   right the children

                                 (pass)

you painting stripes on stairs and circles on chimneys

you under a ceiling open to the sky stencilling walls with stars
                       you, always gesturing towards –

still thinking you have got the trick of this

                         still asking what it will bear

like the shape-shifting snow birds falling and falling upwards

                    lift and lift and lift

Life Sentence

Conceivably, like that precipitate
dream you have, most nights: stepping
out from multi-storey or cliff to leave

your small ant-like pursuers with many
arms raised in forlorn supplication
and breasting the suddenly

buoyant air as if born to be winged.
You explore the lower atmosphere,
swimmingly and in very slow motion:

the earth repels, you foretell your future
off-spring's feathered ankles, effortlessly
revolving arms and obliviousness

to the undertow – till gravity (even in
dreams) rises up to meet you: your feet
at the foot of the heron's droop of your legs,

your pursuers reaching for them, hauling
you down into the street. You contemplate
this leap, the long suspension of it –

the crown, heart cage, fledging appendix.
That dream you have – human.
Its inescapable living weight.

Definition of Huer

(about 288,000 results)

Did you mean: definition of *hue*

Noun. *huer* (plural *huers*) One who cries or gives an alarm.
A balker or conder; one who watches shoals of fish so that they can be caught.

People also ask:
What is a Huer?
Is Huer a Word?
What is the real definition of assailant?
What is the definition of a body part?

Stet

As conservationists tape hairs across a hairline
crack in the plaster as if the house will stand
or fall by them

As someone at her attic desk writes *stick*, then *fracture*,
then erases them

As swifts want vapour-trails, as a plummeting cat twists
in the final foot above the gravel and only a glitch
of the eye says *what was that?*

(so) this summer in parenthesis we are holding our breath
collectively
          also particularly
                    we are failing to connect

was with is,
          in waiting
                    between the here and now
as a writer takes her pen to strike a diagonal through the whole
    (writes *keyboard*
    writes *deletes*
    deletes them)

or someone on the end of a bad line hesitates, not quite
believing what they've heard and says *could you just repeat*
and then with a wry lilt *as you were.*

As if.

In the house that may or may not be falling still someone
writes that all the hairs on the back of the neck bristle.

And there you are in your sand-shoes grinning.

Sometimes I forget you are dead because

as wind runs the length of the roof between slate
and roof-felt with the sough of itself through
large trees or the domino effect

of goods trains sounding out a platform canopy,
interminably – though there are no trains, no planes,
ash, oak, or birches –

so

Also, as wind because it is westerly and windows
front and back were left open yesterday, all
unprepared for a turn in the weather –

so wind that meets the house splits into two
discrete spools: one streaming the gable to lift
corrugated plastic from the lean-to,

the other silk-smoothly unravelling over sleepers'
sleeping forms, along the corridor and out
through the bathroom seamlessly

down the garden path to a space we dream
was park once – wind penned in passing,
wind through leaves –

so

so also

so too

Gone Fishing

First, a shimmy in the silver back of the sea –
    a darker hue that stains the washed-out blue of the water
    and gulls gathered in shoals, a quivering
        fetch at the corner of the eye
        like midges, dust-motes,

or the way I remember you in an orange wool coat
    setting out on the edge of the dark and taking
    the temperature of the air like the ocean.

First, so near-imperceptible an observer high above the bay
    on Hain Walk, eyes sharp as the gulls that just withdraw
    their wings and fall like streaks of white paint –
        or so it seems from here – to vanish
        into the underbelly of the water,

finds himself yelling and brandishing beacons of furze
    scissor-wise over his head before he's understood
    the thing he's seen as shoal or catch or haul:

as when I glance by the wall where they post the names
    of your parish dead and feel the quick of eyes
    that notice me noticing, or when a fish
        senses the sealed surface of its world
        rip open –
                    No.

It's not like this I remember you. Though I could write
    that as the full force of apprehension strikes a split
    second after – so the sign for fish is a man, dancing –

things don't always fall together. A slip, a catch –
     it's not even that. Once we stood on Hain Walk
     and the sign for fish was fish, a body moving
          underwater. Then the thing between us
          twisted and you turned –

I want to say *into the forest*, but what's that about?
     It was your own town you walked out into, late,
     the sea shifty in darkness, in your orange wool coat –

     and if there are signs for that, they don't follow.

Reading *Ane Satyre of the Thrie Estatis* on the Day of the Dead

An craw or ane ke salbe castin up, as it wer his saull – so the playwright wrote, in gall
and lamp-black, in Cupar, in 1540, in small broken-backed minims slanting
upward from left to right as it were the real sea-birds over the firth –

more to the direction than meets the eye, his marks on the page in performance
translating into an open-armed gesture against the sky, sleeve flying wide
and a startled crow or jackdaw winging it, as it were –

The soul implicit.

So too the body in the hospital bed, ended mid-word, mid hand, eyes and mouth
opening as if to recall –

The nurse busy about the curtains and on the lawn

an craw or ane ke stepping out on italic feet: earthbound, investigative.

The window ajar.

So too the gulls off Kenidjack, come mackerel tide, how they just stop dead
and plunge in long white screamers swifter than sight through the slick back
of a wave as needle through silk or thread through invisible needle, their pass

and repass between air and water fluent as it were someone saying on the radio
'not in the world but out there' or that sea bird rapping three times at the glass,
three months on, our quick eye to eye and its turn of the head on the wing, as it were –

Smokey Considers Hilton's Cat

(for Judith, Rufus & Matilda)

It thinks if it keeps close behind the glass
        I shan't notice.

It thinks I've never seen next door's piebald cat
        lie flat between the cherry's shadow-leaves

nor the ginger gentleman Rufus advancing
        through my window up the garden path.

It thinks because I am grey and quiet in my habits
        or because my eyes are amber liquid

it is invisible in its green and red sunspots
        as a mackerel iridescently turning tail.

It thinks I've no knowledge of the laws of opposites,
        no grasp of pixhilation.

It thinks, perhaps, I've never sneezed on glass
        nor sat indoors at night watching my reflection

shot through with headlights heading up from Carn Gloose,
        with the pinpricks of Longships and long houses, boat-like,

or with my own houselights behind me tricking me out
        in an all-over electric halo, sable-tipped,

while I, Smokey, self-coloured cat of Bosavern, sit
        washing a paw, my tail setting a bar

for all the spotty cats of Botallack,
        integer in my fur.

Cot Song

Loose-lipped the lyric falls
    down
        through the leaves singing

its cot-song lullaby like bird-song
    only
        of itself, the sound-

rounded stones and the sky
    invisible
        above the canopy

also some head-turning rock doves
    and choughs
        perhaps topsy in the air

it whistles up for them.
    Non-labial
        lip-service tripping

fulsome off the tongue that is
    not I
        and brooking no – *what?* –

no interruption but tumbling on
    down
        through all its tributaries

to the ocean it sprang from and over
    and again
        so someone at her desk

in a skylit room above the valley
        glancing up
                calls back into the house

'Listen – it's starting to rain.'

Ghost Rhyme

You are under the radar at Land's End, hands
in pockets and laughing like a navigator
back from the war. Your ridiculously long scarf
wraps four times round: chalk pink, dark blue.
        This was thirty years ago.

You are sitting this one out. The small plane
you're not flying has dual controls: when
the pilot manoeuvres left, then right, to lift
off the levers I've not laid finger on shift
        in perfect rhyme

and we sprint comic-strip-style from the cliff
seeing the breakers' frills for the first time as
a matter of life and death: the controller's voice
safe in the ear of the airman who's falling, trying
        to talk him back

across the line. We're flying out above the sky
blue Atlantic, casting off the gorse, the stone hedges
and the house that today I'm writing from, whose tether
of electric, telephone and laundry lines signals to homing
        pilots to begin their final descent –

Up the carn this morning I saw the old radar sounding
the new runway and the skittish little planes that bob
and wheel on the hour, displaying their tail-rhymes
(delta echo xray) as they set off only to return:
        home and dry,

home and away, in a near-perfect likeness
of ending that holds things together casually
as that old dance-hall song you used to sing.

Abstraction

I

There's a house in the trees – white,
with two chimneys. There's a window,

a path that leads across stony ochre
fields to the garden where women

in shades of anemone (scarlet, amethyst)
talk over fences that stand like hieroglyphs

or the scribblings in caves under the cliffs
in whose semaphore war dance the arms,

like the legs, can do anything. Children
with enormous limbs fill the sandpit –

triangulated handkerchiefs for sunhats
and as parachute for their plastic zebra.

Passing trains call through the wood,
gulls endlessly voice their loss. All

these things are the matter – tree-talk
and caves, the racket of the sleepers.

And the lighthouse, invisible from here
but inevitably in the picture as the sea

that rounds it fluently, a riderless horse.

II

He'll start again. There's a house.
He has a wife and two children.

He will have three, and four.
There's a line like a road, a copse

like shadow – no, like the shadowed
cavity between his own finger and thumb.

How quiet it is. The garden's violet
and rose-red plot against a light rectangle

that's the sandpit and the train tracks'
wooden arhythmia: off-white, off-white,

and black. High overhead's the horizon
and a sun golden as the great front wheel

of the tricycle in the future he'll make for
his youngest daughter. In the orchard

someone slowly raises her voice to call
through the branches and a line heavy

with household linen's lifted under
the bleached white canvas of the sky –

He'll start again. He'll paint three apples
in the window: not children, not fallen

worlds, but apples. And that horse: the one
standing darkly by the hedge as if it mattered.

III

There's a white square. A long
dark line. Is this an interior?

That shadowed shadow – a wheel,
or rocking-horse, its nostril?

A dappled dream-horse, breathing
softly in the imagined orchard –

hieroglyph for hieroglyph, things
draw him in. That sketchy V-sign

chalking the square sky marks
both voice and bird, as to his mind

the sense of the vertical beyond
is 'the Light House': the two strong

stresses of it on the hill, out at sea –
both eye and object, impossibly

yoked as when his children danced
and their legs could do anything.

New Year's Day

Because there's no telling them, a solitary
magpie's dropped into the garden by way

of study in binaries. Black and white, open
and shut, but also open and broken:

one wing drags the patio in a slow flat spin.

So too the tilt of a roof that shifts to shine light

on timbers that are growing back to trees and a gable
branching skyward passes the limits of understanding.

[So too my father, re-learning speech through song.]

What hope for things with fault-lines in the joints,
voice taking root, house and wood taking wing?

[...]

The young bird, claws wired in the half-sprung
heart of my palms. Eyes turn and turn about:

the same but different, the same but different again.

New Atlantis

Unthinkable, that what's native to us
as air or its shell's scroll, continuous,
to the hermit crab could be lost –

the familiar contours of town and house
submarine: our stair's spiral a habitat
for barnacles and impediment to sharks,

our night-lights nightly lighting the sea-bed.

Today, when Dunwich bells come tiding
over, we share their tongue still who soon
ourselves will be deeper and further

out than those ladies in pinnacled wimples
of pearl who knew London as *Troy Novant*,
than the legions in fishscale armour marching

up from the coast (then) to name it *Londinium*.

So far out we'll be our words will drift, our
phrases turn senseless
                          she sells sea-shells on the sea

and even this piece of paper in your hand – *hush* –

            unthinkable
                    unth
                            un   n

Look, someone will say, do these primitive signs
stand for waves on the shore? Or do they outline
an aperture – perhaps even some kind of door?

Tailpiece

And so we still go down to the coast
as we still speak the names of our dead
sons, wives and grandmothers that signal
the space they occupied as the first line
of an address raises the house that's gone,
its walls translucent, a light fantastical
through the leaves –

                     the words quick
and shifting, untethered as wild white
horses that gallop silently out to sea,
not fully fleshed, not turning at your call,
not answering to anything.